Screen Hijacked: Break Free from Digital Trap

(A Parent & Adult Guide to Digital Freedom)

By

Swati Chandra

Preface

Screen Hijacked: Break Free from Digital Trap was born out of a simple but powerful realization — our screens are no longer tools we use; they have quietly become the environment we live in. What began as a convenience has slowly evolved into a dependency, quietly shaping our habits, our relationships, and even the way our mind function.

As I watched the world around me — parents overwhelmed by their children's rising screen addiction, adults unable to break free from endless scrolling, families sharing the same room but not the same moments — a truth became impossible to ignore: digital overwhelm has become the modern epidemic we rarely talk about.

This book is not written from a place of judgment, but from understanding. I have seen firsthand how easy it is to slip into the digital trap — the constant notifications, the illusion of connection, the pressure to stay updated, the guilt when we fail to balance it all. And I also know it is not our fault. Our devices are designed to pull us in, to keep us hooked, and to make the digital world feel more urgent than our real lives.

But the good news is this: we can take back control. Not by rejecting technology, but by redefining our relationship with it. Not by unplugging from life, but by reconnecting with it.

Screen Hijacked is written for every parent who feels helpless watching their child drift deeper into screen dependency. It is for every adult who wants to reclaim their time, attention, sleep, and peace. It is for every family longing to bring back conversations, eye contact, and moments that matter.

In these pages, you will find practical guidance, science-backed insights, emotional understanding, and simple actions that create real change. Whether you are dealing with mild overuse, deep digital burnout, or simply want a healthier balance, this book is your companion — not a set of rules, but a roadmap toward digital freedom.

Thank you for picking up this book. Thank you for wanting better — not just for your children, but for yourself.

May this journey help you reclaim the moments you have lost, and protect the ones still ahead.

Welcome to your first step toward digital freedom.

Table of Content

INTRODUCTION – WHEN SCREENS TOOK OVER

There was a time—not too far back—when life felt slower, softer, and more present. Families talked, children played outside until the streetlights blinked on, and adults had long stretched uninterrupted thought. Today, however, silence has been replaced by pings, free time has turned into scrolling time, and human connection competes with glowing screens.

We didn't choose this consciously. Technology didn't invade our life like a storm. Instead, it entered quietly—through notifications, convenience, and curiosity. At first, screens made life easier. Now, for many adults and children, they define life.

Ask yourself:

• Do you check your phone the moment you wake up?
• Do you feel restless when you don't have your device nearby?
• Do you say "just 5 more minutes" and then lose an hour?
• Do your children struggle to stop using screens?
• Do you feel mentally tired despite doing nothing physically exhausting?

If you said yes to even one of these, you're not alone. Families across the world face the same challenges—digital overload, scattered attention, declining conversations, emotional disconnection, and increased anxiety.

Technology is not the enemy. Lack of control is.

This book will not ask you to abandon your phone or disconnect from the world. Instead, it will show you how to:

- use technology without being used by it
- set healthy boundaries
- protect your mental space
- teach children balanced screen habits
- rebuild meaningful family connections
- design a peaceful, focused, intentional life

This is your journey back to control. Your journey back to presence. Your journey to digital freedom.

Let's begin.

CHAPTER 1

THE HIDDEN ARCHITECTURE OF DIGITAL ADDICTION

Technology addiction is not a character flaw. It is the result of **scientifically designed systems** created to keep you hooked. The digital world is not neutral. Everything—from the color of a notification bubble to the speed at which a new video loads—is engineered to capture your attention.

The Illusion of Staying "Connected"

In today's digital world, it feels as if we are more connected than ever before. With a single swipe or tap, we can check on friends across continents, respond to colleagues instantly, watch strangers live their lives, and follow the daily routines of people we barely know. On the surface, it appears that technology has knitted the world closer, making relationships more accessible and communication more convenient. But beneath this comforting illusion lies a truth we often avoid confronting—**we are connected, yet not truly connected.**

Most of our digital interactions are shallow, fragmented, and transactional. A "like" replaces a conversation, a comment takes the place of genuine affection, and a forwarded reel passes off as an expression of care. We have mistaken constant contact for meaningful connection, and in this confusion, the depth of our relationships has quietly thinned.

The illusion becomes stronger because our phones give us constant "social signals." Each notification feels like someone reaching out to us. Every message feels like social warmth. Every tag, mention, or emoji mimic interaction. These micro-gestures trick the brain into believing that emotional needs are being fulfilled. But in reality, most of these signals are algorithm-driven nudges meant to keep us online longer—not genuine human attention.

Despite being surrounded by digital chatter, many people report feeling lonelier, more anxious, and emotionally unsupported than previous generations. Children grow up seeing parents glued to screens, believing that scrolling is the adult version of relaxation. Teens mistake online validation for self-worth. Adults feel pressured to stay updated, fearing that stepping away will disconnect them from the world. Ironically, this race to stay "connected" often distances us from the very people who matter the most.

Real connection requires eye contact, presence, shared experiences, and undivided attention—elements that digital communication rarely provides. A video call cannot replace the warmth of sitting with someone in silence. A WhatsApp message cannot replicate the emotional comfort of a genuine conversation. And no number of followers can compensate for a lack of intimate relationships built on trust and vulnerability.

When we depend on screens to feel connected, we gradually train ourselves to settle for emotional crumbs. We start accepting shallow exchanges as normal, and genuine relationships begin to feel heavy, time-consuming, or inconvenient. The digital world offers quick, easy interactions, but they come without depth. And slowly, without realizing it, we drift into a life filled with people yet surrounded by loneliness.

Recognizing this illusion is the first step toward reclaiming authentic connection. It does not mean abandoning technology—it means using it with awareness. It means choosing to prioritize a ten-minute heartfelt conversation over an hour of scrolling. It means looking at our children when they speak. It means setting down the phone when someone sits beside us. It means reminding ourselves that true connection is built offline, in moments of presence, with people we genuinely care about.

Below are deeper insights into how the digital trap is created -:

1. The Dopamine Trap – How Screens Hijack the Brain

Every time you check your phone, your brain releases **dopamine**, the pleasure chemical.

This creates a loop:

[Trigger] → [Action] → [Reward] → [Repeat]

Notification → Open phone → See "something new" → Feel good

You don't scroll because you're bored—You scroll because your brain expects a reward.

The loop continues—even without notifications. Your brain becomes conditioned to seek micro-doses of happiness. That is why people "check their phone" without a reason.

2. Infinite Scroll – The Feature That Removed Stopping Points

In the past, TV episodes ended. Books had chapters. Magazines had pages.

But social media? It never ends. Apps removed natural stopping points so your brain never hears the signal: *"You're done."*

Your brain stays hooked, thinking the next swipe might bring something better.

3. Notifications – The Digital Doorbell You Can't Ignore

Notifications are not reminders—they are psychological traps.

They trigger:

- urgency
- curiosity
- anxiety

Even the red color of notification icons is intentional—red signals danger and demands attention.

Types of Notifications Designed to Hook You

- *Social pressure:* "Someone liked your photo."
- *Fear of missing out:* "You may know this person."
- *Reward anticipation:* "You have a new follower."
- *Curiosity triggers:* "You won't believe what happened!"

Most are unnecessary—yet impossible to resist.

4. Algorithms – The Invisible Puppeteer

Algorithms study your digital behavior:

- what you click
- what you pause on
- the topics you search
- how long you watch a video
- even what you scroll *past*

Then they build a profile: "What keeps you online the longest?"

And they keep feeding you more of that.

You are not choosing what you see. The system chooses *for* you.

5. Personalization – A Digital Mirror (That You Can't Look Away From)

Your digital world is customized to your:

✓ fears

✓ desires

✓ insecurities

✓ interests

✓ emotions

If you're sad, the algorithm shows sad songs. If you're curious about parenting, it shows parenting videos. If you're insecure about your looks, it shows beauty content and filters. This personalized content makes it almost impossible to disconnect.

6. Variable Rewards – The Gambling Technique Used in Apps

Why do people keep checking their phones even when nothing new is there?

Because the reward is unpredictable. This is the same trick used in slot machines.

Illustration – Variable Reward Cycle

Check phone → Nothing new → Try again

Check phone → Something new! → Dopamine boost

Check phone → Nothing → Try again

The *uncertainty* keeps you addicted.

7. "Free" Apps That Cost You Your Attention

Apps claim to be free. But the truth is: You are the product.

Your:

- time
- patterns
- interests

- emotions
- browsing
- choices

...are sold to advertisers.

The longer you stay online, the more valuable you become.

8. The Illusion of Control – "I Can Stop Anytime"

Most adults believe: "I'm using my phone because I want to."

In reality, many behaviors are not conscious:

- You touch your phone when you're bored.
- You refresh apps without thinking.
- You walk with your phone in hand "just in case."
- You feel uncomfortable without checking it.

This isn't control. It's conditioning. Accepting this truth is the first step toward change.

9. The Emotional Pull – Why Adults Fall Faster Than Kids

Adults may not be playing games or watching cartoons, but they are deeply attached to:

- work messages
- social validation
- online shopping
- news
- inspirational content
- communication
- productivity apps

Many feel:

- responsible
- needed
- appreciated
- connected

…all through their screens.

This emotional connection strengthens dependency.

10. The Silent Takeover – How Screens Become the Center of Life

Screens don't suddenly hijack your routine. The takeover is slow:

- checking notifications first
- replying instantly
- scrolling to relax
- screen during meals
- screen before bed
- screen during conversations
- screen as stress relief

One day you realize— you're living more online than offline.

CHAPTER 2

SCREEN OVERLOAD & ITS IMPACT ON THE MIND

Screens have become our default companion—during meals, travel, work breaks, emotional moments, and even during boredom. Yet what screens *do* to the mind is rarely discussed. The consequences are silent, gradual, and often invisible until they begin interfering with well-being.

This chapter explores how excessive screen exposure impacts the adult mind, the child's developing brain, and emotional health.

1. The Attention Trap — When Focus Becomes Fragmented

In the digital age, our attention is pulled in countless directions at once, leaving the mind constantly juggling unfinished thoughts. Apps are designed to interrupt us—notifications flash, sounds ping, and screens glow—each one demanding a tiny slice of our focus. Over time, these small interruptions splinter our ability to concentrate, making even simple tasks feel heavier and more draining. This constant fragmentation tricks the brain into believing we are being productive because we are always "doing something," yet we rarely complete anything with depth or clarity. The result is a subtle but powerful attention trap: we stay busy but mentally scattered, overstimulated yet under fulfilled. Breaking free begins with realizing that focus is not lost all at once—it is stolen, moment by moment, by every digital distraction we allow in.

Modern screens attack your attention from every angle:

- banner ads
- pop-ups
- autoplay videos
- push notifications
- suggested content
- endless scrolls

Your focus becomes a broken mirror—reflecting everywhere but never staying still.

Illustration: Before & After Attention

Healthy Focus (Before Screens)

[Task → Completion → Reward]

Stable · Clear · Linear · Calm

Screen-Influenced Focus (After Screens)

Task → Notification → Switch → Message →

Update → Scroll → Back to Task → Repeat

This constant switching trains the brain to prefer *short bursts* of attention instead of sustained focus. Over time, adults experience:

- difficulty concentrating
- mental fatigue
- shorter patience
- reduced productivity
- increased procrastination

2. Mental Overload — Too Much Information, Too Little Processing

We consume more information in a day than people 100 years ago did in months. The human brain was never designed for this speed.

Effects of information overload:

- poor memory retention
- confusion between important & unimportant tasks
- decision fatigue

- emotional numbness
- inability to stay present

The mind becomes a crowded room with too many voices speaking at once.

3. Emotional Exhaustion — The Hidden Burnout

Even when you're "resting" on your phone, your mind is working. Scrolling is **not** relaxing—it is stimulation. Your brain processes:

- bright colors
- loud sounds
- fast-moving visuals
- emotional content
- comparisons
- opinions
- conflict

When the mind is overloaded, emotions spiral.

Signs of emotional exhaustion from screens:

- irritation without reason
- anxiety when notifications spike

- feeling drained after scrolling
- emotional oversensitivity
- sadness after consuming negative content

Screens feel like a break—but they break the mind instead.

4. Digital Fog — The New Age Mental Cloudiness

Digital fog is a state where your brain feels:

- slow
- dull
- unfocused
- disconnected
- unclear
- overwhelmed

You may forget simple things or feel mentally "blurry." This comes from *constant mental switching.*

Illustration: Digital Fog Cycle

Overstimulation → Brain Fatigue → Poor Focus → Stress →

More Scrolling → More Overstimulation → Deeper Fatigue

5. Sleep Disturbances — When Screens Steal Rest

Blue light from screens suppresses **melatonin**, the sleep hormone. Even 10 minutes of screen use before bed can delay sleep by 45 minutes.

Sleep-side effects:

- trouble falling asleep
- shallow sleep
- morning tiredness
- less REM sleep
- increased nightmares or vivid dreams

Children are affected even more deeply because their brains are still developing.

6. Adults Are Affected More Than They Believe

Adults often lie to themselves:

"I only use my phone for important things."

"I scroll to relax."

"I can stop anytime."

But studies show adults spend MORE non-productive screen time than children.

Reasons include:

- work emails create guilt
- social media creates pressure
- online shopping creates excitement
- news creates urgency
- notifications create anxiety

Screens quietly hijack adult minds without them realizing it.

7. The Disconnect Between Real Life & Screen Life

Screens trick the brain into believing:

- quick entertainment equals real happiness
- online productivity equals real accomplishment
- online socializing equals real relationships

But nothing digital can replace:

- eye contact
- real conversations
- silence
- nature

- physical presence
- emotional depth

When screen life grows, real life shrinks.

CHAPTER 3

WHEN SCREENS REPLACE HUMAN CONNECTION

Homes today often look like this:

A family sitting together, but each person scrolling.
A child trying to talk while a parent types a message.
A couple sharing a bed but not sharing conversations.
Friends meeting but taking photos instead of enjoying the moment.

Screens haven't just taken our time—they've taken our relationships.

When screens begin to fill the emotional spaces meant for real people, our relationships quietly shift from warm and meaningful to distant and mechanical. We start choosing quick messages over heartfelt conversations, emojis over expressions, and online updates over genuine presence. Slowly, the people right beside us become background figures while the digital world takes center stage. This replacement feels convenient, even efficient, but it leaves a growing emptiness—because no screen, no matter how advanced, can offer the comfort of eye contact, the reassurance of a soft voice, or the healing power of shared silence. When screens take the place of human connection, we stay "connected," yet feel more alone than ever.

1. The "Alone Together" Reality

Today, families often sit in the same room yet live in completely different worlds—each person absorbed in their own screen, their own feed, their own digital bubble. This is the "Alone Together" reality: physically present but emotionally distant. We share space, but not moments. We sit beside each other, yet drift further apart as our attention is pulled inward by glowing screens. What feels like peaceful coexistence slowly becomes silent disconnection, where real conversations fade and genuine bonding becomes rare. In this digital quietness, loneliness grows not from being alone, but from being surrounded by people who are no longer fully present.

People are physically close but emotionally distant.

Illustration:

Family on Sofa:

[Parent → Screen]

[Child → Screen]

[Teen → Screen]

[Guest → Screen]

Everyone is "together," yet each person is in a different digital world.

2. Conversations Shrink, Emotions Shrink Too

When our daily exchanges are reduced to short texts, quick replies, and hurried voice notes, our emotional world begins to shrink alongside them. Screens encourage brief interactions, not deeper conversations, and over time we lose the habit of expressing what we truly feel. Children stop sharing their worries, adults stop opening up, and families slowly drift into emotional silence. When conversations become shorter, our capacity for empathy, patience, and understanding gradually fades. Real emotions need space—something digital conversations rarely provide. And when that space disappears, connection weakens, and our emotional bonds grow thinner without us even noticing.

Screen habits reduce:

- eye contact
- meaningful conversations
- active listening

- emotional sharing
- empathy

Real conversations become:

- shorter
- distracted
- shallow
- rushed

This weakens relationships over time.

3. Children Compete with Screens for Attention

In many homes today, children find themselves silently competing with screens for their parents' attention. A child's question, laughter, or tiny accomplishment can easily go unnoticed when an adult is absorbed in a phone. Over time, kids learn to speak less, interrupt less, and expect less—not because their needs have changed, but because they feel overshadowed by a device that always seems more urgent. This unintentional neglect leaves a deeper impact than we realize. When children feel unheard or unseen, their confidence, emotional security, and sense of belonging slowly erode. They don't need perfect parents—they just need present ones. And presence begins the moment the screen is set aside.

A child's heart learns from the parent's eyes. When those eyes are constantly on a device, children feel:

- unimportant
- unheard
- emotionally disconnected

This creates behavioral issues:

- tantrums
- attention-seeking
- anger
- sadness
- withdrawal

4. Digital Validation Replaces Real Connection

In a world driven by likes, shares, and comments, many people begin to measure their worth through screens instead of through genuine human relationships. A heart emoji soon feels more comforting than a real conversation, and the approval of strangers online starts to matter more than the presence of loved ones at home. This shift is subtle but powerful—emotional needs that were once met through warmth, touch, and understanding are now replaced by digital symbols and fleeting reactions. While online validation feels immediate, it lacks depth, creating a hollow sense of connection. The more we chase this digital approval, the further we drift from the authentic relationships that truly nourish our emotional wellbeing.

Adults and teens chase:

- likes
- comments
- shares
- appreciation
- online applause

But online validation is temporary. Real connection comes from presence.

5. The Loss of Family Rituals

Family rituals—once the anchors of togetherness—are slowly fading as screens take center stage in daily life. Meals that were once filled with conversation are now spent scrolling, and bedtime stories are replaced by videos that never ask for eye contact or connection. Simple traditions like evening walks, weekend games, or shared prayers quietly disappear as everyone slips into their separate digital worlds. These rituals may seem small, but they are the threads that hold families close. When they vanish, the sense of belonging weakens, and moments that once created memories are replaced by silent scrolling. Reclaiming these rituals isn't just about reducing screen time—it's about restoring the heartbeat of family life.

Traditional bonding moments fade:

- bedtime stories replaced by videos
- family meals replaced by mobile screens
- outdoor activities replaced by online entertainment

These losses weaken emotional closeness.

6. The New Form of Loneliness

Loneliness today is not being alone. It is being surrounded by people who are not mentally present.

Despite being constantly surrounded by digital noise, many people today experience a quiet, unfamiliar loneliness—one that doesn't come from being alone, but from being emotionally disconnected. We scroll through updates, watch others live their lives, and stay plugged into endless conversations, yet still feel unseen and untouched. This new form of loneliness hides behind busy screens and full notifications, masking an inner emptiness that technology cannot fill. It grows when real conversations shrink, when eye contact fades, and when our emotional needs are replaced by digital distractions. True connection requires presence, vulnerability, and human warmth—ingredients no screen can replicate.

Digital loneliness is silent yet painful.

CHAPTER 4

THE PARENT'S DILEMMA — RAISING CHILDREN IN A DIGITAL WORLD

Modern parents face a challenge no previous generation ever encountered: raising children in a world where screens are everywhere, irresistible, and deeply woven into daily life. While technology offers learning, entertainment, and convenience, it also introduces risks that are often invisible until the damage is done—shortened attention spans, emotional withdrawal, sleep disruption, and a dependence on digital validation. Parents are caught between wanting to protect their children and not wanting them to feel left out, between encouraging healthy tech use and resisting the overwhelming pressure of the online world. This is the heart of the dilemma: how to raise grounded, present, emotionally connected children while navigating a digital environment designed to pull them away. It's a daily balancing act filled with guilt, concern, and countless tough choices—but awareness is the first step toward doing it with confidence and clarity.

Parents today are the first generation required to manage children + technology. There is no handbook. There are no past examples. There are no clear rules. You are learning as you go.

1. Children Mirror Adult Behavior

Children learn far more from what they see than from what they are told. When adults constantly check their phones, scroll during conversations, or turn to screens for comfort, children naturally adopt the same habits. They begin to believe that devices deserve the same attention as people—or sometimes even more. Over time, a child's sense of normal shifts: family time includes screens, meals involve scrolling, and quiet moments are filled with digital noise. This mirroring isn't intentional, but it is powerful. When children observe adults choosing screens over connection, they learn to do the same. The most meaningful way to teach healthy digital behavior is not through rules alone, but through the example we set every single day.

Children do not learn digital habits from lectures; they learn from what they see. If parents:

- use phones during meals
- scroll while talking
- check notifications constantly

Kids absorb this as "normal."

2. The Digital Gap — Kids Move Faster Than Parents

In today's world, children adapt to technology with astonishing speed, often outpacing the adults trying to guide them. While parents are still learning the basics of new apps or platforms, kids have already mastered them, discovered shortcuts, and moved on to the next trend. This widening digital gap can leave parents feeling overwhelmed, unsure, or even powerless. Children, meanwhile, navigate online spaces with confidence but without the maturity to understand the risks. This imbalance creates a silent vulnerability—kids move quickly, but without guardrails; parents want to protect, but struggle to keep up. Bridging this gap requires open dialogue, continuous learning, and the courage to stay involved even when the digital world feels intimidating. This gap leads to:

- confusion
- arguments
- lack of understanding
- miscommunication

3. Behavioral Signs of Screen Dependency in Kids

Screen dependency in children often begins quietly, showing up through subtle behavior changes that become stronger over time. A child who once enjoyed outdoor play may start resisting activities that don't involve a device. Irritability, restlessness, or emotional outbursts when the screen is taken away are early red flags. You may notice them rushing through meals, chores, or conversations just to get back to a game or video. Their patience shortens, attention wanders, and real-world interactions start feeling "boring" compared to the constant stimulation of screens. These behavioral shifts aren't signs of laziness or defiance—they're indicators that a child's brain is becoming conditioned to seek digital reward, and gentle intervention is needed before dependency deepens.

- Irritability when the screen is removed
- Inability to play independently
- Poor attention
- Lack of interest in offline activities
- Emotional outbursts
- Reduced imagination
- Constant boredom

4. Healthy vs. Unhealthy Screen Use

Healthy Use

Healthy screen use means enjoying technology in a balanced and mindful way. It includes using screens for learning, creativity, and communication while taking regular breaks, sitting in a comfortable posture, and stopping when the eyes or mind feel tired. Healthy habits help us stay focused, relaxed, and in control of our time. Examples of healthy uses are-:

- learning
- creativity
- educational videos
- supervised games
- time-limited use

Unhealthy Use

Unhealthy screen use happens when screens take away time from sleep, physical activity, family, or hobbies. It may also include endless scrolling, gaming for long hours, or using devices late at night. When screen time becomes uncontrolled, it can lead to stress, eye strain, and difficulty concentrating. Examples of unhealthy uses are-:

- addictive games
- endless videos
- scrolling for hours
- exposure to harmful content
- emotional dependence

5. The Emotional Risk for Children

Children growing up in a digital world face emotional risks that often go unnoticed. Constant exposure to screens can make them more sensitive to online feedback and less confident in their real-life interactions. When their self-worth becomes tied to likes, comments, or virtual achievements, it can create anxiety, frustration, or feelings of inadequacy. Excessive screen time may also limit opportunities to develop empathy, patience, and emotional resilience—skills that grow through face-to-face conversations and shared experiences. As children rely more on digital spaces for comfort or distraction, they may struggle to understand and express their emotions in healthy ways. Recognizing these risks helps parents guide their children toward a more balanced emotional foundation.

Screens can damage:

- self-esteem
- emotional regulation
- body image
- sense of identity
- social skills

Early prevention is easier than reversing damage.

CHAPTER 5

HIDDEN RISKS BEHIND THE SCREEN

Behind every glowing screen lies a world of invisible risks that quietly shape our thoughts, habits, and emotions. What appears to be harmless entertainment or quick information often masks powerful algorithms designed to capture attention and influence behavior. Children and adults may unknowingly absorb unrealistic standards, harmful content, or subtle pressure to keep scrolling, leading to stress, comparison, and emotional fatigue. The constant stream of notifications can trigger anxiety, interrupt real-life moments, and weaken our ability to stay present. These risks rarely show themselves instantly—they build slowly, hidden beneath convenience and connection—making it essential to recognize what the screen takes away even as it gives so much.

Digital risks are real—even when they seem invisible.

1. Cyberbullying

Cyberbullying has become one of the most painful consequences of growing up in a digital world. Unlike traditional bullying, it doesn't stop at the school gate—it follows children home, appearing on their screens at any hour, through hurtful messages, exclusion, rumors, or public shaming. The anonymity of the online space often gives bullies the courage to say things they would never dare say face-to-face, making the impact even more damaging. For children, these digital wounds can trigger deep emotional distress, fear, and isolation, especially because the audience is no longer limited to a few classmates but potentially thousands. Understanding cyberbullying is essential, not only to protect children but also to teach them empathy, responsibility, and the power of using technology with kindness.

Children may face:

- insults
- exclusion
- threats
- humiliation
- anonymous harassment

Impact can be severe:

- anxiety
- depression

- withdrawal
- fear

2. Online Predators

Online predators are one of the most frightening hidden dangers behind screens, often disguising themselves as friends, mentors, or peers to gain a child's trust. They create emotional connections through flattery, attention, or shared interests, slowly lowering a child's guard. Because predators operate from behind digital identities, children may not recognize warning signs until they are deeply entangled in a harmful relationship. These interactions can lead to manipulation, emotional exploitation, coercion, and, in severe cases, attempts to meet in person. The most troubling part is that predators are skilled at targeting children who feel lonely, misunderstood, or unheard. Understanding how these individuals operate is crucial for parents—it empowers them to educate their children, recognize early red flags, and intervene before trust is misused or safety is compromised.

Predators disguise themselves as:

- friends
- gamers
- fellow students

- friendly adults

Children must learn:

- never to share personal information
- never to talk to strangers online
- to report anything uncomfortable

3. Gaming Addiction

Gaming addiction is a growing concern in the digital age, where immersive graphics, instant rewards, and competitive challenges keep children—and even adults—glued to their screens for hours. What often begins as harmless entertainment can slowly turn into a compulsive habit, where the virtual world becomes more appealing than real-life responsibilities. Children may lose interest in studies, outdoor play, or family interactions as they chase higher scores, new levels, or social validation from online gaming communities. Over time, the constant stimulation rewires the brain's reward pathways, making it harder for them to stop even when they want to. This addiction can lead to emotional instability, irritability, sleep disturbances, and a decline in overall well-being. Recognizing gaming addiction early is key, because healthy limits and balanced routines can restore control before the game begins controlling the child.

Gaming can worsen:

- sleep
- academic performance
- emotional health
- physical activity
- attention
- social interaction

4. Social Media Comparison

Social media comparison is one of the most subtle yet emotionally damaging effects of the digital world. As children and adults scroll through endless streams of perfectly edited photos and carefully curated moments, they begin to measure their real lives against someone else's highlight reel. This constant comparison quietly chips away at self-esteem, making ordinary days feel inadequate and personal achievements seem small. For children, who are still discovering who they are, these unrealistic standards can create pressure to look a certain way, behave a certain way, or live a life that isn't actually theirs. Over time, this comparison trap can breed insecurity, jealousy, anxiety, and a sense of never being "enough." Recognizing this invisible influence is essential, because understanding the difference between real life and digital illusion helps free the mind from unnecessary emotional burdens.

Children believe:

- filtered photos = reality
- edited lifestyles = normal
- online perfection = goal

This damages self-worth.

5. In-App Purchases & Money Exploitation

In-app purchases have quietly become one of the most manipulative elements of the digital world, especially for children who may not fully understand the value of money. Many apps and games are designed with psychological triggers—limited-time offers, bonus rewards, flashy animations—to nudge young users into spending without thinking. What begins as a small purchase for a new skin, character, or upgrade can quickly turn into repeated, impulsive buying. For parents, this often results in unexpected bills and confusion about how the spending happened in the first place. Behind the scenes, companies deliberately craft these features to keep children engaged and spending more, blurring the line between entertainment and exploitation. Teaching kids to recognize these tactics and setting clear digital boundaries is essential to preventing emotional manipulation and financial harm.

Games intentionally create:

- frustration
- progression blocks
- tempting upgrades

Kids learn unhealthy money habits early.

CHAPTER 6

BUILDING DIGITAL DISCIPLINE AT HOME

Building digital discipline at home is not about strict rules or constant monitoring—it's about creating a healthy, respectful relationship with technology that the entire family follows together. Children naturally mirror what they see, so when parents model balanced screen use, mindful habits, and device-free moments, kids learn to do the same. Digital discipline grows from small, consistent practices: fixed screen schedules, no-phone zones during meals, shared tech-free evenings, and open conversations about online safety. Instead of relying on fear or punishment, the focus shifts to teaching responsibility—helping children understand *why* limits matter and how screen habits affect their mood, sleep, and relationships. When families work as a team, digital discipline becomes a shared lifestyle rather than a daily battle, creating a home where screens support life instead of stealing it.

Creating balance requires a family system, not individual effort.

1. Create Family Screen Rules

Creating family screen rules is one of the most effective ways to bring clarity and balance to digital life at home. Instead of vague expectations or sudden restrictions, clear rules set a shared foundation that everyone—children and adults—can follow with confidence. These rules may include designated screen-free times, limits on gaming or social media, device curfews, and guidelines for safe online behavior. When the entire family participates in setting these rules, children feel included rather than controlled, making them more willing to cooperate. Consistency is key; rules should apply to everyone, not just kids, so the message of fairness and teamwork stays strong. With well-defined agreements in place, screens become tools rather than distractions, helping families protect their time, relationships, and emotional well-being.

Examples:

- no screens during meals
- 1–2 hours max daily
- devices off by 8 PM
- no phones in bedrooms
- weekend screen breaks

2. Create Tech-Free Zones

Creating tech-free zones at home is a powerful way to reclaim spaces for real connection, calmness, and presence. These intentional areas—whether it's the dining table, bedrooms, or a cozy corner in the living room—serve as gentle reminders that not every moment needs to be shared with a screen. When families designate these spaces, they create opportunities for unhurried conversations, mindful relaxation, and uninterrupted bonding. Children benefit enormously from seeing that certain parts of the home are reserved for rest, creativity, or quality time, not digital noise. Tech-free zones also help reduce overstimulation, improve sleep quality, and encourage healthier habits without constant conflict. Over time, these screen-free pockets become safe, peaceful sanctuaries where family life can breathe again.

3. Involve Children in Rule-Making

Involving children in rule-making transforms screen guidelines from rigid commands into shared agreements they feel responsible for. When kids have a voice in shaping the boundaries—like deciding screen-free hours, choosing family activities, or helping set gaming limits—they are far more likely to follow them willingly. This collaborative approach helps children understand *why* limits exist instead of seeing them as punishments. It also strengthens trust, boosts confidence, and teaches essential life skills like negotiation, responsibility, and self-control. By treating children as partners in the process, parents create a family culture where digital boundaries feel fair, respectful, and easier to maintain. Ultimately, rule-making becomes a team effort rather than a source of conflict, encouraging healthier relationships with screens for everyone.

Ask them:

- what rules feel fair
- what times are best for screens
- what consequences are reasonable

Participation increases cooperation.

4. Replace Screens with Activities

Replacing screens with meaningful activities is one of the most effective ways to shift children's focus from passive consumption to active engagement. Instead of simply saying "no screens," offering appealing alternatives—like art projects, puzzles, outdoor play, reading, cooking, or family games—helps children discover new passions and develop important skills. These hands-on experiences stimulate creativity, strengthen family bonds, and encourage healthier emotional expression. When children experience the joy of real-life activities, the pull of screens naturally weakens, making digital limits feel less restrictive and more balanced. Over time, these screen-free moments build richer memories, strengthen resilience, and remind children that fulfillment doesn't come from pixels but from experiences that engage the mind, body, and heart.

- puzzles
- reading
- outdoor play
- music
- creative arts
- family games

CHAPTER 7

THE 21-DAY DIGITAL FREEDOM CHALLENGE

The 21-Day Digital Freedom Challenge is a simple yet transformative journey designed to gently reset your family's relationship with technology. Instead of abrupt restrictions, this challenge introduces small daily steps that gradually reduce dependency and build healthier digital habits. Each day focuses on one mindful action—whether it's a tech-free meal, a screen-free hour, a gratitude practice, or a family activity that replaces digital noise with real connection. By spreading these changes over 21 days, families experience a steady shift: improved focus, better sleep, calmer moods, and deeper interactions. What makes the challenge powerful is its practicality—any parent, child, or adult can follow it without feeling overwhelmed. At the end of three weeks, screens no longer control the home; instead, families regain clarity, balance, and the confidence to use technology with intention rather than impulse.

A step-by-step transformation journey.

Week 1: Awareness (Days 1–7)

The first seven days of the Digital Freedom Challenge focus on building awareness—because you cannot change what you do not recognize. During this phase, families simply observe their screen habits without judgment. This includes noticing when screens are used the most, what triggers the urge to check devices, and how digital use affects mood, sleep, and relationships. Parents and children track their patterns, reflect on how screens shape their routines, and identify areas that feel stressful or out of balance. These early days are about honesty, not restriction—creating a clear picture of what needs to improve. By the end of week one, families understand their digital habits more deeply and feel prepared to make meaningful, lasting changes in the weeks ahead.

- track screen time
- observe emotional triggers
- identify addictive apps
- separate essential vs. non-essential digital tasks

Week 2: Reduction (Days 8–14)

- disable notifications
- delete time-wasting apps
- limit social media to 20 minutes
- create a morning and night routine

- replace scrolling with meaningful tasks

Week 3: Balance (Days 15–21)

- practice mindful phone use
- schedule digital breaks
- take one offline day
- engage in offline hobbies
- journal your progress

CHAPTER 8

REWIRING YOUR BRAIN FOR BETTER FOCUS

In today's fast digital environment, our minds have been trained to jump from one notification to another, making focus feel almost impossible. Yet the human brain is incredibly adaptable, and with the right habits, it can be reshaped to concentrate better. This chapter explores how intentional routines—like practicing deep breathing, reducing multitasking, taking screen breaks, and engaging in slow, mindful activities—gradually rebuild attention strength. When we give our brain moments of silence, make space for offline hobbies, and replace constant scrolling with purposeful actions, we create new neural patterns that support clarity and focus. Rewiring the brain is a journey of small daily choices that help us shift from distraction-driven living to a more centered and productive state of mind.

1. Mindful Phone Usage

Mindful phone usage is about taking back control from automatic habits and turning every interaction with our device into a conscious choice. Instead of picking up the phone the moment we feel bored, lonely, or curious, this approach encourages us to pause and ask, *"Why am I using it right now?"* By setting clear intentions—such as checking messages only during fixed time slots, disabling unnecessary alerts, and avoiding phone use during meals or conversations—we create healthier boundaries. Mindfulness also invites us to notice how certain apps make us feel and to replace draining screen time with more nourishing activities. Over time, these small awareness-based decisions reduce impulsive scrolling, lower mental clutter, and help our brain rebuild the ability to focus on what truly matters.

Before checking your phone, ask:

- Why am I picking this up?
- What do I need right now?
- Is this necessary?

2. Deep-Work Intervals

Deep-work intervals are focused pockets of time dedicated to one meaningful task without the interruption of screens, messages, or multitasking. By working in short, structured bursts—such as 20, 30, or 45 minutes—we teach the brain to stay engaged for longer stretches and improve concentration. During these intervals, distractions are removed: phones are placed out of sight, social media tabs are closed, and the mind is guided toward a single goal. The key is not perfection, but consistency; even a few deep-work sessions a day can strengthen attention muscles and reduce dependency on digital stimulation. Over time, these planned focus periods help break the cycle of constant interruptions and allow the brain to rediscover the satisfaction of undivided effort and genuine productivity.

Start with 10 minutes of uninterrupted focus. Increase gradually to 45 minutes.

3. Replace Distracting Apps

One powerful step toward building stronger focus is to replace distracting apps with tools that support personal growth and calmness. Many digital platforms are designed to steal attention through endless feeds, loud notifications, and emotional triggers. By identifying the apps that drain time—social media, addictive games, or constant news updates—and swapping them for healthier alternatives, we shift how the brain uses technology. Educational apps, digital planners, meditation tools, or music platforms for concentration can offer value without overwhelming the mind. This change not only reduces mindless scrolling, but also rewires daily routines, proving that the phone can be a resource rather than a trap. Over time, this conscious replacement builds discipline, supports productivity, and frees mental space for deeper, more rewarding experiences.

Use apps for:

- reading
- meditation
- learning
- habit tracking

4. The One-Screen Rule

The One-Screen Rule encourages using only one device at a time, instead of juggling multiple screens that compete for attention. Many people watch TV while scrolling on their phone or work on a laptop while replying to messages, unknowingly splitting their focus and tiring the brain. By choosing to stick to a single screen, we reduce cognitive overload and give our mind a chance to stay present with what we are doing. This simple rule teaches the brain to follow one task from start to finish, strengthening patience and attention span. Over time, this practice becomes a habit and helps replace chaotic multitasking with a calmer, more organized rhythm, allowing us to enjoy digital technology without losing control to constant distraction.

Only one screen at a time:

- no phone while watching TV
- no second screen during work
- no multitasking apps

CHAPTER 9
CREATING A BALANCED TECH-LIFE ROUTINE

Creating a balanced tech-life routine is about using technology in a way that supports life rather than replaces it. This balance begins with understanding how much time screens genuinely deserve and how much time should be reserved for real-world activities. Setting practical limits—like screen-free mornings, device-free meals, or a digital curfew before bedtime—helps the mind reset and strengthens focus. It also encourages space for exercise, hobbies, relationships, and quiet moments that screens often push aside. A balanced routine does not demand giving up technology; instead, it teaches us to use it intentionally and meaningfully. When digital habits align with personal goals instead of constant entertainment, life feels calmer, richer, and far more productive, allowing screens to become tools rather than masters.

Routines bring stability.

1. Digital Morning (0–60 minutes device-free)

Starting the day without screens for the first 60 minutes gives the mind a chance to wake up naturally, without being pulled into messages, social media, or news alerts. This simple habit protects the brain from an early rush of information and emotional triggers that can shape the whole day. A device-free morning allows room for peaceful routines—stretching, planning the day, journaling, eating breakfast, or simply sitting quietly with thoughts. During this time, the brain shifts from autopilot scrolling to intentional thinking, setting a calm, focused tone. Over days and weeks, this practice strengthens emotional balance, lowers digital cravings, and reminds us that life begins with ourselves—not with a screen.

2. Digital Night Routine

A digital night routine focuses on gradually disconnecting from screens to help the brain and body slow down before sleep. As evening approaches, reducing exposure to bright screens, social media conversations, and fast-paced content allows the mind to shift out of alert mode. Creating a simple ritual—like dimming lights, reading a book, reflecting on the day, or spending quiet time with family—signals the brain that it is time to rest. Avoiding screens at least 30 to 60 minutes before bedtime improves sleep quality, reduces mental noise, and prevents late-night overstimulation. Over time, this routine becomes a calming anchor, turning nights into moments of recovery rather than chaotic scrolling, and supporting better focus and emotional balance for the next day.

- **Set a "Screen Cut-Off Time"**
  Decide a specific time every night to stop all digital use—messages, TV, calls, and scrolling. This builds discipline and consistency.

- **Reduce Blue-Light Exposure**
  Explain how blue light from screens interferes with melatonin production, making it harder to sleep and recharge mentally.

- **Create a Relaxation Ritual**
  Encourage calming activities like reading, meditation, warm baths, or stretching to replace screen time.

- **Keep Devices Outside the Bedroom**
  Discuss the benefits of charging phones in another room to reduce temptation and night-time interruptions.

- **Avoid Emotional or Stressful Content**
  Consuming intense news or social feeds before bed can trigger anxiety and racing thoughts, harming sleep.

- **Journal Your Day**
  Reflecting on the day's achievements and worries can empty the mind and improve emotional regulation.

- **Prepare for Tomorrow Offline**
  Use a physical planner or notebook to list next-day tasks rather than checking digital reminders at night.

- **Create a Low-Stimulation Environment**
  Dim lights, reduce noise, and keep the bedroom cool to support deep, restorative sleep.

- **Practice Digital Silence**
  Talk about the power of spending the last hour in quiet, without music, videos, or endless scrolling.

- **Teach Kids by Example**
  For parents, modelling healthy night routines helps children avoid screen addiction and understand balance.

3. Weekend Digital Detox

A weekend digital detox is a powerful way to reset the mind and break away from the constant pull of screens. Families and individuals can choose a format that suits their lifestyle—whether it is switching off devices for half a day, dedicating one full day, or committing to alternate Sundays with no digital interruptions. Even a half-day break creates breathing space to reconnect with hobbies, nature, conversation, and personal goals without digital noise. A full day offers deeper benefits, allowing the brain to rest from information overload and rediscover simple joys like board games, cooking, or outdoor activities. Following alternate Sundays builds a long-term rhythm where the mind learns to look forward to screen-free time rather than fear it. These intentional breaks reduce digital dependence, strengthen relationships, and remind us that real life happens beyond the screen's glow.

4. Social Media Boundaries

Social media boundaries are essential for protecting mental space, emotional balance, and personal time in a world where online platforms are designed to hold our attention. By choosing specific moments to check apps instead of scrolling throughout the day, we prevent digital interruptions from taking over work, study, and family life. Limiting uploads helps reduce the pressure of constant sharing and allows real experiences to stay personal, while avoiding mindless browsing protects hours of the day from being lost to endless feeds. Staying away from late-night scrolling also supports better sleep and calmer thoughts. These simple boundaries turn social media into a controlled tool rather than a constant distraction, helping individuals stay connected without sacrificing peace, productivity, or focus.

- **Check Only During Specific Times**
  Scheduling social media use for fixed times during the day helps regain control over attention. Instead of opening apps every few minutes, planned check-ins—perhaps morning, afternoon, and evening—create structure and reduce impulsive scrolling. This approach prevents social platforms from interrupting studies, work, conversations, and real-life interactions. When social media is accessed intentionally, the brain learns to stay focused on tasks without expecting constant digital stimulation. Over time, this habit builds discipline, lowers digital anxiety, and allows social media to exist as a small part of life, not the centre of it.

- **No Late-Night Scrolling**
  Late-night scrolling disrupts sleep, heightens mental activity, and fills the mind with unnecessary comparisons and emotional triggers. Avoiding social media during night hours gives the brain a chance to wind down

naturally and prepares the body for quality rest. Without the blue light and fast content that overstimulate the mind, people fall asleep faster and wake up clearer and calmer. This rule also protects emotional health because night-time scrolling can intensify loneliness, jealousy, or negative thinking. Replacing it with calming routines like reading or reflection turns nights into peaceful recovery time rather than online chaos.

- **No Mindless Browsing**
  Mindless browsing is the silent thief of time and attention. It happens when we scroll without purpose—often out of boredom, habit, or emotional escape. Setting the boundary of "no mindless browsing" encourages people to open apps only with a clear reason, like replying to messages, checking updates, or sharing something meaningful. This shift reduces wasted hours and strengthens self-awareness. It also helps people notice emotional triggers behind automatic scrolling—stress, loneliness, procrastination, or curiosity. By eliminating purposeless browsing, social media becomes a conscious tool rather than a reflex, giving space for creativity, hobbies, and deeper real-world engagement.

- **Limit Uploads**
  Limiting uploads helps reduce the pressure to constantly document life for online approval.

When sharing becomes intentional instead of frequent, people stop chasing likes and validation and reconnect with real experiences. Uploading less also protects privacy, reduces comparison, and keeps boundaries between personal life and public display. This practice teaches that meaningful memories do not always need to be posted—and living in the moment carries more emotional value than capturing everything for the internet. Over time, limited uploads foster confidence, authenticity, and a healthier relationship with social media.

CHAPTER 10

RECONNECTING WITH THE REAL WORLD

Reconnecting with the real world is about rediscovering the beauty, depth, and meaning that exist beyond digital screens. When we intentionally step into offline life—talking face-to-face, exploring nature, reading physical books, creating art, cooking, or simply observing the world around us—we awaken senses that technology often dulls. Real-world engagement builds emotional strength, empathy, patience, and stronger relationships, because it invites genuine human connection rather than virtual reactions. It also slows life down, allowing thoughts to settle and creativity to grow. By shifting attention from curated online lives to authentic lived experiences, we remind ourselves that joy, identity, and purpose are found in presence, not scrolling. Reconnecting with the real world creates space for deeper living and helps us rebuild a healthier, grounded relationship with technology.

Screens take you away from real experiences.

1. Strengthen Relationships

Strengthening relationships begins with being fully present and choosing real connection over digital distraction. Having meaningful conversations allows people to share emotions, ideas, and stories that deepen trust and understanding. Active listening—paying full attention without planning replies or checking phones—helps others feel valued and heard. Asking thoughtful questions shows genuine interest and keeps discussions rich and personal, encouraging stronger emotional bonds. Spending device-free time together, whether during meals, family activities, or quiet evenings, creates shared memories and restores warmth that screens often replace. These simple habits rebuild human closeness, reminding us that relationships grow through presence, curiosity, and time—not through likes and comments.

2. Rebuild Old Hobbies

Rebuilding old hobbies is a powerful way to reconnect with passions that may have been pushed aside by digital distractions. Activities like painting, gardening, writing, playing a musical instrument, or crafting not only bring joy but also engage the mind in creative and fulfilling ways. Revisiting hobbies encourages patience, focus, and a sense of accomplishment that constant screen use rarely provides. It also offers a healthy break from technology, allowing the brain to rest while nurturing personal growth and self-expression. By making time for these familiar interests, we reclaim a part of ourselves, strengthen our identity beyond digital lives, and create meaningful, screen-free moments that enrich everyday living.

3. Reduce Digital Noise

Reducing digital noise is essential for regaining focus, calm, and control in a world overflowing with notifications, alerts, and constant online updates. By turning off unnecessary notifications, unsubscribing from irrelevant emails, and limiting app alerts, we can prevent our attention from being hijacked every few minutes. This also includes curating social media feeds to remove distracting or negative content and choosing only the platforms that add real value. Reducing digital noise creates mental space for reflection, creativity, and meaningful tasks, allowing the brain to concentrate on what truly matters. Over time, it fosters a calmer, more intentional digital life where technology serves us, rather than constantly demanding our attention.

CHAPTER 11

TEACHING LIFE SKILLS TO KIDS OUTSIDE DEVICES

Teaching life skills to kids beyond screens is crucial for their holistic growth, independence, and emotional intelligence. While digital tools can provide information, real-world experiences nurture problem-solving, empathy, creativity, and resilience in ways no device can replicate. Simple activities like cooking, gardening, budgeting, fixing things, or collaborative play teach responsibility, patience, and critical thinking. Encouraging children to interact with peers, nature, and family members helps them develop social skills, emotional awareness, and a sense of community. By guiding kids to learn through hands-on experiences and challenges outside the digital realm, parents equip them with essential skills to navigate life confidently, think creatively, and build meaningful connections that screens alone cannot provide.

Screens cannot replace essential life skills.

1. Social Skills

Teaching social skills to children is essential for building strong relationships and emotional intelligence. Simple practices like maintaining eye contact help kids convey confidence and attentiveness, while encouraging clear and respectful communication enables them to express thoughts and feelings effectively. Involving children in teamwork—through group activities, games, or collaborative projects—teaches cooperation, problem-solving, and shared responsibility. Cultivating empathy, by helping them understand and consider others' emotions, nurtures kindness and compassion. Together, these skills equip children to navigate social situations with confidence, connect meaningfully with others, and develop the emotional awareness needed for lifelong personal and professional success.

2. Emotional Skills

Helping children develop emotional skills is essential for their mental well-being and healthy relationships. Teaching kids to recognize and name emotions like anger, sadness, frustration, joy, and fear allows them to understand their inner experiences and respond thoughtfully rather than react impulsively. Activities such as discussing feelings, journaling, role-playing, or simply talking about daily experiences can guide children in identifying these emotions. When children become aware of their emotional states, they learn self-regulation, empathy, and problem-solving, which strengthens resilience and social interactions. Developing emotional literacy early equips kids with the tools to navigate challenges calmly and build a balanced, confident sense of self.

3. Real-World Skills

Teaching children real-world skills prepares them for independence and responsibility in everyday life. Simple tasks such as cleaning, organizing personal spaces, cooking easy meals, and helping with household chores teach practical abilities while fostering discipline and confidence. These activities also instill a sense of contribution and teamwork within the family, showing kids that their efforts matter. Learning hands-on skills nurtures problem-solving, time management, and self-reliance, helping children feel capable and prepared for real-life challenges. By practicing these skills consistently, kids gain both competence and pride in their abilities, building a strong foundation for adulthood.

4. Creative Skills

Developing creative skills is vital for nurturing imagination, problem-solving, and self-expression in children. Activities like drawing and crafting allow them to visualize ideas and explore their artistic side, while storytelling encourages language development, critical thinking, and empathy by imagining different perspectives. Engaging with music—whether singing, playing instruments, or listening mindfully—stimulates memory, coordination, and emotional awareness. Encouraging these creative outlets not only provides fun and enjoyment but also strengthens confidence and innovative thinking. By incorporating creative activities into daily routines, children learn to express themselves freely, think outside the box, and develop a lifelong appreciation for arts and culture.

CHAPTER 12

BECOMING A DIGITAL ROLE MODEL

Becoming a digital role model means demonstrating healthy, intentional, and responsible use of technology, especially for children, peers, and those who look up to us. It goes beyond limiting screen time for oneself; it involves showing balance, mindfulness, and respect in online interactions. By practicing conscious phone use, avoiding impulsive scrolling, and prioritizing real-life connections, adults set a powerful example that influences younger minds and peers alike. Sharing thoughtful content, engaging positively on social media, and modeling offline activities reinforce lessons of discipline, empathy, and digital responsibility. Ultimately, being a digital role model helps create a culture where technology supports growth and connection rather than distraction and stress, inspiring others to make mindful choices in their own digital lives.

Children become who they observe.

1. Practice the Behaviors You Expect

Practicing the behaviors you expect from others, especially children, is one of the most effective ways to model healthy digital habits. Simple actions like keeping your phone away during meals demonstrate the importance of presence and undivided attention in family interactions. Avoiding phone addiction by setting personal limits shows that balance is achievable and necessary. Managing notifications—turning off unnecessary alerts or prioritizing important messages—reinforces control over technology rather than being controlled by it. Exhibiting discipline consistently, whether by taking screen breaks, sticking to planned phone usage, or engaging in offline activities, sends a powerful message: healthy digital habits are not just rules, but a way of life worth following. By embodying these behaviors, we guide others to adopt similar practices naturally and effectively.

2. Be Present

Being present means fully engaging with the moment and the people around you, rather than letting screens and digital distractions dominate attention. It involves consciously listening during conversations, noticing surroundings, and immersing oneself in activities without constantly checking phones or devices. Practicing presence strengthens relationships, enhances focus, and allows for richer experiences, whether during family time, work, or personal hobbies. When we choose to be mindful and attentive, we model this behavior for others, showing that real-life connections and experiences are more valuable than digital interruptions. Over time, cultivating presence nurtures calmness, clarity, and deeper appreciation for everyday moments.

3. Explain, Don't Just Enforce

Children are more likely to adopt healthy digital habits when they understand the reasons behind rules rather than following them blindly. Explaining the "why" helps kids see the purpose of boundaries, such as limiting screen time, avoiding late-night scrolling, or choosing device-free activities. When they grasp the benefits—better focus, improved sleep, stronger relationships, and emotional balance—they are motivated to cooperate willingly. Sharing reasoning also encourages critical thinking, reflection, and discussion, transforming rules from strict commands into meaningful lessons. By explaining instead of simply enforcing, parents and educators foster understanding, responsibility, and long-lasting habits that children are more likely to internalize and carry into adulthood.

4. Protect Family Time

Protecting family time means intentionally creating moments that are free from screens and digital distractions, allowing members to connect deeply and meaningfully. Simple practices like device-free meals, weekend activities, or dedicated family evenings foster communication, trust, and shared experiences. When technology is consciously set aside, children and adults alike feel valued, heard, and supported, strengthening emotional bonds. Protecting these moments also teaches kids the importance of presence and prioritizing relationships over constant connectivity. By establishing consistent, distraction-free family time, households cultivate warmth, understanding, and memories that screens can never replace, reinforcing the sense of togetherness that is essential for healthy, balanced lives.

CONCLUSION

YOUR DIGITAL FREEDOM STARTS NOW

You now hold the tools to reclaim your time, mental clarity, relationships, and emotional balance. The goal is not to reject technology but to rise above it—to use it with awareness, intention, and confidence.

Digital freedom is not a one-time choice. It is a daily practice.

Start small. Stay consistent.

Give yourself and your family the gift of presence.

Your life belongs to you—not your screen. And today, you take that power back.

Appendix

WORKSHEET 1: Digital Self-Assessment (Adults)

Instructions: Circle the option that best represents your current behavior.

1. How often do you check your phone first thing in the morning?

☐ Always

☐ Often

☐ Sometimes

☐ Rarely

☐ Never

2. Do you use screens to escape stress or boredom?

☐ Yes, frequently

☐ Occasionally

☐ Rarely

☐ Never

3. Do you feel anxious when you can't check your phone?

☐ Yes

☐ A little

☐ Not sure

☐ No

4. How many hours a day do you spend on your phone?

☐ 1–2 hours

☐ 3–4 hours

☐ 5–6 hours

☐ 7+ hours

☐ I don't know (calculate below)

5. Which apps consume most of your time?

(write your top 5)

1. ______________________________
2. ______________________________
3. ______________________________
4. ______________________________
5. ______________________________

WORKSHEET 2: Digital Profile Mapping

Purpose: Understand what triggers your device usage.

Trigger	My Reaction	How It Makes Me Feel	Healthier Alternative
Stress	Check phone / scroll	Tired, distracted	Deep breathing / walk
Boredom	______________	______________	______________
Loneliness	______________	______________	______________
Habit	______________	______________	______________
Notifications	______________	______________	______________

Add your own rows as needed.

WORKSHEET 3: Screen Time Tracking Chart (7 Days)

Week of: ______________________

Day Total Screen Time Productive Use Unproductive Use Notes

Monday ____________ ____________ ____________ _________

Tuesday ____________ ____________ ____________ _______

Wednesday ____________ ____________ ____________ ______

Thursday ____________ ____________ ____________ ______

Friday ____________ ____________ ____________ ________

Saturday ____________ ____________ ____________ _______

Sunday ____________ ____________ ____________ ________

WORKSHEET 4: Phone-Free Zones Planning Sheet

List the areas in your home and the rules for each.

Area / Activity	Current Habit	New Rule	Start Date
Dining table	Phones allowed	No screens during meals	________
Bedroom	Phone next to bed	Charging outside room	________
Family time	TV + phones	Family hour – screens off	________
Homework	Phone often nearby	Silent + away from desk	________

Add more rows as needed.

WORKSHEET 5: My Digital Boundaries (Adults)

Fill in your new habits:

1. Morning Screen Rule:
Before phone, I will:

____

2. Work Screen Rule:
I will check messages only at:

____

3. Social Media Limit:
I will use social media for: __________ minutes per day

4. Night Screen Rule:
My cut-off time is: ____________________

5. Replacing Screen Time With:
(choose 3 activities)

☐ Reading

☐ Journaling

☐ Walking

☐ Meditation

☐ Hobby (insert) ___________________

☐ Family time

☐ Cooking

☐ Exercise

WORKSHEET 6: Child Screen Behavior Observation Sheet

Use this as a weekly evaluation tool.

Behavior	Yes	Sometimes	No
Child gets irritated when asked to stop screen	☐	☐	☐
Prefers screens over outdoor play	☐	☐	☐
Easily distracted during homework due to device	☐	☐	☐
Sleeps late because of screen	☐	☐	☐
Watches content beyond age-appropriateness	☐	☐	☐
Engages in creative, non-screen activities	☐	☐	☐

WORKSHEET 7: Family Digital Harmony Plan

We agree to:

1. **Screen-free mornings until:**

   ____

2. **Screen-free meals:** Yes / No (circle)
3. **No phones in bedrooms:** Yes / No
4. **Family time (1 hour) daily at:**

   ____

5. **Weekend digital detox activity:**

   ____

Family signatures:

Parent: ________________

Parent: ________________

Child: _________________

Child: _________________

WORKSHEET 8: Digital Detox Blueprint (3-Day or 7-Day Plan)

Day 1 – Reduce

Apps to hide/mute/remove:

Day 2 – Replace

Screen time replaced with:

Day 3 – Reclaim

Old habits I want to rebuild:

For 7-Day Detox, extend the list to 7 sections.

WORKSHEET 9: Mindful Usage Reflection Log

Use this after a day of intentional digital habits.

1. What helped me reduce screen time today?

____

2. What challenges did I face?

____

3. What emotion was behind my screen use?

☐ Stress ☐ Anxiety ☐ Habit ☐ Boredom ☐ Comparison

☐ Other: ____________________________

4. What will I improve tomorrow?

____

____

WORKSHEET 10: Device Inventory Sheet

List all devices and their rules.

Device	Who Uses It?	Purpose	Rules / Limits
Smartphone	Parent	Work/Personal	2 hours social media
Tablet	Child	Learning	Allowed only with supervision
Laptop	Parent	Work	No work after 9 PM
TV	Family	Entertainment	Max 1 hour/day

WORKSHEET 11: Content Quality Evaluation (Kids & Adults)

Before consuming content, check the boxes:

☐ Is this content educational?

☐ Will this help me grow in any way?

☐ Will I feel good after watching/reading it?

☐ Is it age-appropriate?

☐ Is it safe? (no violence, negativity, adult content)

☐ Am I watching because I WANT to, not out of habit?

If you check fewer than 3 boxes → *Reconsider watching.*

WORKSHEET 12: The "Before You Scroll" Pause Test

Ask these questions before picking up your phone:

1. What am I picking up my phone for?

____

2. How long do I plan to use it?

____

3. What emotion am I feeling right now?
☐ Bored ☐ Stressed ☐ Lonely ☐ Curious ☐ Habit
☐ Other: ______________________

4. Is there something better I can do instead?

____

Checklists

CHECKLIST 1: Healthy Screen Habits for Adults

☐ Phone stays outside the bedroom

☐ Social media checked only twice a day

☐ App notifications turned off

☐ Work boundaries set

☐ Daily "no-screen zone" time

☐ Replacement activities planned

☐ Night-time screen cut-off followed

☐ Mindful breaks every 1–2 hours

☐ Weekly digital detox practiced

CHECKLIST 2: Healthy Screen Habits for Kids

☐ Set screen time limit

☐ Educational content prioritized

☐ NO screens during meals

☐ NO screens 1 hour before bed

☐ Outdoor play included

☐ Digital chores chart followed

☐ Parental controls enabled

☐ Content supervised

☐ Screens used only in shared spaces

CHECKLIST 3: Digital Detox Weekend

☐ Plan one outdoor activity

☐ Turn off social apps

☐ Keep phone in another room

☐ Zero screens before breakfast

☐ Try a creative offline hobby

☐ Spend 1 hour in nature

☐ Family board game night

CHECKLIST 4: Phone Decluttering

☐ Delete unused apps

☐ Unfollow negative accounts

☐ Remove addictive games

☐ Mute noisy group chats

☐ Limit push notifications

☐ Organize home screen

CHECKLIST 5: Productivity Boost Checklist

☐ Use Do Not Disturb during work

☐ Create a daily top-3 tasks list

☐ Block distracting sites

☐ Use timer-based work blocks

☐ Keep phone in another room

CHECKLIST 6: Screen-Free Home Setup

☐ Charging station outside bedrooms

☐ Screens stay out of dining area

☐ Books/magazines placed in visible corners

☐ Family activity shelf created

CHECKLIST 7: Social Media Minimalism

☐ 10-minute daily limit

☐ Weekly unfollow routine

☐ Remove time-wasting apps from home screen

☐ Prioritize value-based accounts

CHECKLIST 8: Mental Well-being Screen Reset

☐ 5-minute breathing before screen

☐ 20-20-20 eye rule

☐ 10-minute break after 60 minutes

☐ Zero screens when overwhelmed

CHECKLIST 9: Work-Life Digital Balance

☐ No work messages post-dinner

☐ Fixed hours for checking emails

☐ Keep work device separate

☐ Weekend digital rest

CHECKLIST 10: Emergency Screen Plan for Kids

☐ Pre-decided screen rules

☐ Offline activity basket ready

☐ Timer set before usage

☐ Calm communication scripts

www.ingramcontent.com/pod-product-compliance
Lightning Source LLC
Chambersburg PA
CBHW062111160726
48282CB00026B/757
9789356079007